ROYAL SILKS

The woman sits in her zinc tub
on the marble floor. Beside her,
an ewer of English pottery
festooned with roses. On a low table
are her soaps, a loofah, a pumice stone.
She reaches for the ewer of hot water,
her breasts are pale moths
in the dusky light. Water spills,
gathers in small pools where a turquoise tile
shuts the open drain. Under the floor,
water curdles like leper skin.

The morning is a story book,
slow telling of lungur in the trees,
Benares silk, kitchen smells
of coriander and ginger.
In the bathing room, the woman stands,
rivulets of water run down.
She steps onto the wooden mat,
dries, dusts talcum powder
in the pier glass mirror.

The room is large. A breeze floats
through as the punkah disturbs
the tropic air. The blind punkah wallah
sits in shadow, a cord tied to his toe.
He sits and sits and pulls the punkah
through the air.

But today it is not the blind man
who sits, for he is in his village sick, a
charpoy under a banyan tree.
His seeing brother sits here instead,
eyes open in the shaded marble by the bath.
The woman leaves the room, glances
at the rose petal ewer, the thick towels,
her image in the pier glass mirror.

The punkah wallah sees and she does not
that she is not alone. Her shadow
shrinks under her feet, her shallow skin,
as she passes through the door.

PATIALA

The old manservant sits
in a corner in the dark room but
you do not see him. You enter
the unlit hall, sheen of framed
photographs on dull panelled walls.
You pass through the dining-room,
its mass of table, high-backed
chairs, chandelier like fireflies
in the cold space.

Quick light, the library door opens,
an electric heater presses near
four upholstered chairs, a red-
eyed guard dog. Awkwardness.
Your host and his friend indicate
your place, pour out Indian whisky,
taste of rice and sweet molasses.

You talk of a time in summer
long ago, the watered lawns,
tents of striped imperial canvas,
beautiful women, the men in royal
silks, uniforms with red jackets,
or the perfect white of cricket.
A long silence, a knock. A tray,
the door shuts silently

and you eat curry fragrant with
coriander, cinnamon bark, fenugreek.
Basmati rice perfumes the leather
and dusty-shelves smell of the room,
warms your body untouched by
weak fingers of electric fire.

After coffee, you are taken into
reception rooms, lights switched
on and off as you pass, reading
the walls, their photographs of silken
rajahs, gem stones and peacocks,
polo ponies, trophies, palaces as white
and delicate as wedding cakes.

Now you are very cold, the ice
of the mountains creeps around your feet,
around the photographs of dead tigers
in jungle sunlight, elephants,
thousands of birds in neat
lines in a garden. The men with
guns, the memsahibs elsewhere,
the servants obedient and dark.

When it is time, you drink
a ceremonial last whisky, the books
remote and empty on the shelves.
You say your thanks, goodnights,
again are led through the dining-room.
The light from the library door trails
across the hall where a pile of rags
on the floor is only the old servant,
rubbing polish into the dark wood.

Wild elephants forage through the park at night.
Where they stop to drink, their feet leave
plump footprints in the river mud. Mist
weaves a shawl over their browsing.

Sometimes, grasses and leaves
are not enough, restlessness
comes over the elephants. Then,
a great male, remembering
the wild hillsides of youth,
leads the herd out of the park.
They come into the tea estate
where coffee berries ripen
under the shade of orange trees,
on a Feast Day now for elephants.
They pluck the coffee bushes
with their agile trunks, shake
the trees and the fruit falls
ready on the ground.

All night they savour delicacies,
bread fruit, berries and sweet oranges.
In the morning, the plantation manager
from Goa, white hair
like ocean waves at Trivandrum,
calls the park director.

Out of the park, the tame elephants
approach, their legs in chains, obedient.
Now they are vigilantes, will round up
thieves, march them back
to gazetted confines of park.

And some night soon when leopards prowl,
when the park director sleeps
and the plantation manager drinks
Portuguese wine in the town,
the wild elephants will roam again,
eyes alert in the starlight,
trunks probing the scented
air, to dine on oranges
in the coffee glade.

A green so light, not jade, not sky.
Ice water rushed out of the Himalayan
silence into this wide scarred channel.

Along the other shore ashrams
are seashell-coloured, beige,
cream, coral, sea green.

The pilgrims who wash on the flooded steps
emerge new from the sacred waters.
They are transfigured in scarlet,

saffron, emerald. Even the birds
are blessed with such colour.
The kingfisher is as royal

as any prince, his *gazi* a white-fronted
waterhen in grey and russet.
Now the song, rich as honey,

of the black-headed oriole
calling pilgrims out of the dry land.
This benediction of water, overflowing.

As many gods are here, as many devotees
as specks of sun-lit dust rising
from a cremation ghat.

The sun sets on the other side
of the ridge, high and narrow
as bones. Wind in the deodars,
night fingers in the grass.

An old man at home
among tombstones coughs,
guarding this graveyard
of foreign dead.

Courteously, he asks
passers-by for medicine
as if death were a curable disease;
they, eager for dinner, climb
away from the contagious damp,
a barbet calling.

The old man sucks his breath
with difficulty, as if it too came
from his neighbours.
As he settles into night
his neighbours take from him
even the sound of his sleep,
death and silence
imperious and familiar.

Our car stranded
and my husband gone in a taxi somewhere
looking for gas:
the Mediterranean a flat blue omelet
under the glass bowl of sky.

I am sitting on an iron chair
by the roadside waiting,
sipping a thick, sweet cup
of Turkish coffee. A child calls
plaintively, "Anne, Anne, Anne."
The kiosk radio broadcasts misfortune,
but this is no misfortune for me.
In the long spring grass yellow daisies
praise the sun, wave boldly
in the sea wind. Cars go by
on the narrow asphalt road.
The gold-toothed man in the kiosk
brings me another coffee, the news is over
on the radio. A woman sings
of love, "Canım, Canım," and
says he will never return.

I am waiting on the Antalya road
passionate for this day,
the yellow sun, the olive trees,
an old man in black shalvar
waiting for a bus, the strong earth
pushing up spring grass,
so much life
that is not mine.

The rickshaw wallahs jog around
the mountain, the shaded, perfumed
forests sound the valleys far below.
In the rickshaws, families sit comfortably
together, each proud father looks out,
spanning the horizon with his glance.
His wife is wrapped in pink or green chiffon;
her gold bracelets ring like temple bells.
Between them the son, as plump and sweet
as freshly made *gulab jamun*, a new toy held
tightly to his chest. This is all.
The daughters do not exist, are little
memories their mothers weep for
when they are alone, moths fluttering
in a star-filled jar.

This tropical night of stars and blossoms
we forage the tennis courts for moths
sucked here by light.
They cling along the netting
like fossils, or dried fruit
of some now withered vine.

The moths are fragile,
sombre-hued and still.
Hand-in-hand like this
together we seek their cryptic art.

We have company in our explorations,
small grey lizards on the netting
silent, sudden. Thin prowling cats.
Minute ants on the trail
of a victim: they look for moths
to make a dinner of

and we also look for moths
to spend this hour after dinner,
to linger in the gracious air
and something more:
there is a secret here
beyond the hunger
and the delicate moths.

I reach out:
only fine powder
dusty on my finger tips.

SUTTEE

Greetings …
… the answer must be …
I have never forgotten …
    1888 cylinder recording
    attributed to Queen Victoria

By that time, twenty-five years of black
mourning robes had consumed me.
The voice recording device,
I spoke into it one morning because
it would have amused Albert, my husband,
and I wished I had his voice still
speaking to me, even on a wax cylinder,
the way he speaks to me every day
in my heart, in the faces
of my children.

I never forget Albert, even for a minute,
although it is now my Jubilee,
and I should be remembering
that Coronation Day before Albert,
my robes, my Crown: garments
I have grown into slowly,
learning the power of the Throne
and the men who came to me for permission.
That there is more than mother, or nuptial bed,
to being Queen, and why Disraeli
proclaimed me Empress of India.

I saw it as a gold cloud studded with gems,
men of many colours kneeling, their silken robes.
Pearls and rubies, tracts of forest and savanna
wider than the ocean. I could imagine
music and the sound of heathen voices,
moonlit palaces, but never the smell,
the dense air, the diseases which sent men
home as yellow, desiccated ghosts.

I have never forgotten the dark face
of that woman brought to Court, her silk
robes of yellow gold, her eyes ringed
with black, and the red disk in the centre
of her forehead. She rang out as she walked,
her gold anklets and bracelets, and the thick
odour of sandalwood oil.

In my drawing-room, I heard her story.
She was a widow, condemned to burning
on her husband's funeral pyre.
Suttee, she called it, faithful wife.

"I have escaped," she said.
"My sisters lie beside
their husbands like tinder."

She was as an animal in the Royal
Zoological Gardens, a creature
strange and shocking.
I have never forgotten when she walked
into my room, how she flared
as she said, "Greetings."

They called it *chotta hazari*, "little breakfast," those
pine-scented years when my husband was a boy. The bearer
carried it in on a tray before the sun was up. Bananas, an
orange, the teapot covered with a knitted cozy, hot milk
boiled on a charcoal stove. Now, this morning in Simla,
those years are alive again, the waiter knocks and enters
with a tray. His black hands flitter like birds as he sets
down with the care a priest gives to the sacrament each
object. Cup, spoon, sugar bowl, teapot, boiled milk under
its wrinkled skin. When he tilts the pot, when his gnarled
hands pour tea into white cups, feathered time binds his
world to ours, even to the orderly movement of the seasons
and the stars.

WRITTEN UNDER BARK

We met William at the wooden gate where the Welsh hills fall
to the Rheidol River. He was herding sheep into a new field,
Cass and Sally cutting them off, dropping to the grass when he
called out, "Lie down Sal. Cass, lie down!" Together we climbed
the hill, followed William through the muddy door to the
kitchen.

"I was in Canada in the War," William says. His long
white moustaches curl valiantly, his blue eyes are
open as the sky. The smell of sheep drifts in from
the field-green doorway.

"Bloody cold place. Then I got transferred out to the Coast. I
was in Vancouver that time they flew two squadrons of Kitty
Hawks over the Rockies and lost them all. Froze up,
they did." He pours water into the fat brown tea pot.
"One time I saw a Japanese sub chasing a fish boat, attacked
with my rear gunner firing, maybe scratched their paint. So I
looked around for something to drop, and there were just
these kit bags looking a bit like depth charges.

"So I threw one out, it wasn't mine, you can be sure.
That sub dived that fast. Headlines in the paper next day,
bright red, says RAF SINKS JAP SUB. I was that embarrassed,
felt like a stupid bugger. The brass just wanted some good
news, didn't matter if it was true or not. They even said I was
up for a medal." Our questions, unasked, hang in the air.

He takes the cups from a shelf. "No woman tells me what to do. I live as I please," William says and looks at the kitchen wall piled high with wood split for the iron stove, Sally and Cass, his dogs, soft-eyed in their wide boxes by the door.

Through the doorway, we watch the sheep like fat white grubs on dancers' legs. They scamper down the long grass hill, stand staring back, their black and white faces harlequin masks.

PIGEONS

Pigeons in London have been observed
hopping on "the tube" and getting
around the capital by underground in
seemingly organized fashion.

News Report.

The tourists flock from America,
Japan, South Africa, to stand
in Trafalgar Square, their
outstretched hands alight
with pigeons, and do not suspect

these lavender birds are guests
newly arrived, ship stow-aways
or marathon aviators
from colonies far away,
here to see the sight
of people milling on the stones
under Lord Nelson's stare.

The strut and coo of red-eyed
suitors is more open and seductive
than a brown-eyed Lothario
in his Spanish clothes. Oh see
Cyrano, his pigeon poems
drooping like lilac feathers.

His avian peers crowd to
hear the pigeon Marco Polo
boast of night adventures
in a Siam courtyard, soon
eagerly depart to Euston Station,
Tottenham Court Road
for assignations beneath
the web of bridges, tower
stones, or bill and coo
under the hooded eaves.

Behind the window, travellers
dream of lovers in feathered jackets,
the soft murmur of first love.

KINGSTON

May, 1989

In the garden, trees plucked
clean by hurricane
struggle to resume their shade.
We sip good Jamaican coffee:
breakfast on the Club verandah
where vervain hummingbirds
buzz borders of opulent flowers.
New wind stirs our tablecloth.

In Peking students are awake
watching in Tiananmen Square.
Here, the poor are waking to rice,
yams, a little salt fish.

Listen.
Bob Marley is telling you about it.

daggers of hot sun
cutting the traffic
black man
white dust
he holds out his hand
empty

On the terrace of Devon House
iced lime juice
tinkles cool in glasses.
A black woman
arranges flowers
(she learned this in Singapore)
for a party of chartered accountants'
wives.

agapanthus
(blue suns in a shaded bowl)
palm leaf fans
gladioli like pink kimonos

Her finale is a low dish:
green leaves doubled into sails,
orange parrot lilies like calligraphy.
For this she receives
her paid applause.

LAKI PENAN

Sarawak

At Long Lamai in the Upper Baram
at Ba Ajeng, at Long Beruang
from Suai, Niah, Bintulu
the Penan retreat into their forest, until
the trees fall, the jungle
shudders and dies

we are like fish thrown on the land
the Penan say
when sago palms are killed
when jack fruit are killed
when animals are killed
for what shall we live?

we stand at the roadblock until we die

but what can blowpipes do when
iron hornbills come out of the sky?
we are the short-tailed macaques
          the long-tailed macaques

we are afraid

For a little while, we walk through the forest
carrying our beads, our cloths, our blowpipes.
In the forest is our food, our clothing
our shelter, our medicine.
The sound of the nose flute is sweet
beside the clear-running water

Protect our ancestors and ourselves
we pray   to the gods of the Christians
             to the gods of the Muslims
             to the old gods at the *bale kebutan*

what can they do?
the owl calls out at night
the hornbill calls in the morning

his feathers rattle like beans in an empty gourd

SHALIMAR HOTEL

Kuala Lumpur

It was not falling water,
those notes from the grand
piano in the lounge although

water was falling, outside
beyond the transparent wall,
among the banana trees

and the travellers' palms.
Young girls like orchids
offered tea or coffee,

their butterfly limbs
kneeling, as thin as stems.
It was as if the silence

of water falling outside
was also in their eyes,
the touch on china
of their hands.

I was telling the story of the Kitty Hawks,
those planes that might or might not have
disappeared over the Rockies
in the War, and Connie
who is listening, says, "I remember the
Kitty Hawks, the rumours that year."
She stares out into the garden.
"We were all eighteen, a bunch of girls
in uniform waiting for something exciting
to happen. There was a sergeant in Operations
in Esquimalt, he had been a mechanic.
Retooled a shop so they could work
on the Kitty Hawks. It was hushed up,
he said. His friends told him six went down.
Later, I heard two squadrons."

After lunch I went looking for Connie.
She was sitting on the verandah
among baskets and boxes of flowers,
petunias, lobelia, red spice geraniums.
A circle of hot sun spinning
from her coffee cup sat like a butterfly
on the ceiling.

"That's all I can tell you," she says.
"We were so young, a long time ago.
But I remember the sergeant saying,
You know the way boys with nothing better to do
on a cold Prairie morning, maybe forty below,
scare starlings out of a barn.
Those birds fly for a few seconds, then drop
out of the air, frozen to stones.
That's the way they say those planes went down."

Froze and fell like dead birds, Connie repeats.
Each pilot seeing the Rockies
for the first time.

TREE RINGS

One

The tomb of King Midas is half-
exposed, under its tumulus on the dry
sweep of Anatolia. His golden hoard
gone, but the Lebanon cedars, more
durable than wealth, hold up
the roof with arms of giants.

The close-grown fibres
within the beams are histories,
can tell how many chariot years
have ridden the plain since Midas died.
But the trees do not record
great battles, songs of minstrels
in fountained gardens. Here
are the bones of history,
the hard account of drought
and plenty, volcano and fire.
Do not ask of them
the colour of King Midas' cloak,
how beautiful his many wives
nor the number in thousands
of his slaves.

The trees will tell you only
when the peasants starved and when
the wheat was golden in the granaries.

Two

The ancient Caren forest
has its feet in ice, slow
progression into vigour
while great glaciers retreated
ten thousand years ago.
Generations of sub-alpine kings
lean into history or rot
under thick sphagnum moss,
transcribing soil to tumuli.

Here, two thousand year old
trees are history books.
Who else wrote the sun and moon
before Malaspina sailed the paddled,
cloud-stained straits
below steep-sided Texada Island?
Before Vancouver named the Caren Range,
carrying the Empire's banner
even to this outlandish shore:
the history of the natives
of this place, of wind, of sun,
the burning fire, are written
under bark.

Do you remember that when we crossed
the border on foot, the guards
would not let us pass? It was cold,
I wore my black beret. We sat in a small
room as if we were guerrillas.
They were sorry to let us go.
That night in the third class carriage,
wooden seats and an indescribable toilet,
there were two men from Pamplona.
We were homesick for Canada, we had never
been to Spain. The men shared a loaf
of homemade bread, it had a red sausage
baked inside. One had a bottle of rosé
enclosed in a gold-coloured net. Outside,
an endless plain. Together we sang songs
all night, New Year's Eve.
The others in the carriage were drunk
or asleep. In the morning,
how could we ever meet again?

Thirty years ago, do you remember?
A car bomb exploded today in San Sebastian,
the Basque separatists still slip across
the border with death in their baggage.
The two men from Pamplona are old now,
perhaps they sometimes sit in the sun,
drink wine, sing with their neighbours
the songs of Pamplona. I remember
that we clasped hands for a long time
before we parted.

My husband has a sister who
remembers everything.
She sits in a corner of the sofa and pulls
memories from her handbag untarnished,
accurate in every particular.

She remembers Mrs. B. who came
to care for the children
after Mother died, the glassed
rooms at the front and the far away
storms rising over the Indian Plains.
She remembers Gordon, eighteen,
taking the rooms for himself
while the draped bedroom ceiling
gradually lowered with dust sifted
through from the floor upstairs.
She remembers a long time before this
when Gordon sent Sylvia skidding
downhill on a silver tea tray.
Sylvia lay unconscious under a tree
for hours, and they were afraid
to tell.

I have listened so long to these stories
that I smell the dust,
know the gleam and shape of the tea tray,
hear the laughing-thrushes in the trees outside.
When my husband's sister
crossing a darkened room
feels a mouse run over her foot,
I know that she has spilt
India ink on the floor,
see where it has splashed, indelible
on the bare wood boards.

It happens like this. Sometimes
you go on a long journey
and your arrival is smoke
and mirrors, you cannot decipher
the taste of the night.
Coyote empties the air.

Now, you stand in a window
on the third floor
with the implausible expectation
that all horizons are sea.
As if mermaids were singing somewhere.
Here, in the shell of your ear,
wind calls the name of snow.

The small child in you then
runs home. Ravens
clack at the sun, break
a black flight like ink on glaze.
The heart of the cedar remembers you.
Yellow-eyed, the eagle from the high
snag takes you in. Here
in this dream you are
    where you want to be
    who you want to be.

The huckleberry breeze is your breathing,
the wild currant bush is your cloak.
Seven times the otter whistles your name.

In low tide shallows the sun
gives back your face.

It was like a periscope you
looked into backwards,
the X-ray in the shoe store.
Where you put your foot,
you could see a picture,
the skin peeled back, the flesh:
white bones in a blue haze
on the bottom of the sea.

We thought kids lucky
who lived in town;
on their way home from school
each day, they got to look.
They fought for turns to gaze
at peerless symmetry of bones
under their dusty socks, scuffed shoes,
pale familiar skin.

Once my mother pondered
half an hour over the black dress pump
or the patent leather sandal
(which the clerk knew all along
she wouldn't buy). Then,
I stared uninterrupted
at a new perfection.
In that blue gulf unicellular
beginnings swam into fishes,
climbed the shore, stood upright,
became I.

The children from the town have grown,
their skeletons accreted, elongated,
hardened under the pale, familiar skin.
Some have paid forfeit
for the vision of bones
(dangerous knowledge outside the garden).

Roots reach out,
hidden; another symmetry
within the bleak,
secluded earth.

ANCESTORS

An old man walks in the park
not regularly, but from time to time
the way you glimpse an idea
at the edge of your mind

You see him among the dark
trees in the park,
his slippers quiet as smoke
on the narrow path,
his beard as thin as if
a brush had been dipped
in rain water

When he is gone you forget
that you have observed him,
but while he is passing
you remember pictures
of ancestors in blue
embroidered brocade,
a temple where incense burns
in the eye of a dragon

You remember a bowl
on an altar, pears
as green as winter wheat,
as round as the moon.
You remember that you did not
belong in the temple, that outside
the rain was warm and heavy
as blankets

You remember that an acolyte
gave you one of the pears,
that when you bit into it,
it was rough and sweet
as the air in a foreign country

When the old man has passed
through, the park is familiar,
the air smells of earthworms.
Dull yellow maple leaves
paper the winter grass.

He talks about forests all the time.
In the morning I pick pine needles
out of my breakfast cereal,
listen to the crash of harvest licences.
At lunch, my friend's latest bon mot is
buried under an avalanche
of falling firs.
Our bed is a vast clearcut,
our pillows full of sawdust.
When I inadvertently start a story
about a bear on a logging road,
it is swept away in the undertow
of watershed destruction.

My favourite words, salmon, cedar, snow
are kept hidden and locked.

I have to defend myself against a crime
I am not committing. I am a stand-in
for everyone who buys a morning newspaper.
I want to scream like a seagull,
fly out to the far kelp beds.

Every old cedar that falls, the damp earth,
the crushed salal, speak to me too.
I keep trying to say this.

I keep trying to say, all I need is
a piece of paper small enough
to write this down.

I gather memories like seashells
and set them in a box of scented cedar
wood. My fingers stain with berries
as I work. I hold my breath
and listen to the night.
Small creatures rustle under the shallal.

When my father was away at night
my mother told us stories. Like berries
they fell onto our plate. Cedar
logs cracked softly. Smoke like breath
drifted among the trees. Shallal
instead of garden, and seashells.

For six days my father cut shallal,
my mother said. Her hands were stained with cedar.
As she swelled with my new self her breath
was sweet and soft as berries.
She listened in the night
to sea rhythms. Seashells

marked her garden paths. Seashells
shone between the cosmos and shallal.
My father cleared the cedar
bush to build a house. His breath
came hard with pick and axe. Nights
and quiet rest, a rosary of berries.

The wood stove was good for pies. Blackberry
was his pleasure. Through shallal
my gentle mother carried water. Cedar
kindling and her breath
created fire. At night the sea shelled
dreams, the honest, well-earned night.

For a babe there is no break of night
from day. I slept within the cedar-
smelling house. No need for me to bury
memory now, it is soft breath,
love which shimmers like seashells,
a garden under moon and dark shallal.

So I will praise red berries and shallal,
a quiet house sleeping, cedar
smoke hallowing the night.

ALONG THE WATER PATHS

i   Glaciers retreating, dropping
    walls of rock crushed into water
                   silted with time

    slowly clearing, lakes opening
    water-rush
    over gravel
    an arduous trail from the sea   like silver

    like silver, bright-eyed
    along the water paths

ii Fisherfolk say salmon are oilier
    in Johnstone Strait

    at the mouth of the Fraser
    swimming, rivers and lakes
    channels, rapids, deep water
    already the fasting, losing
    flesh

    at last absorbing even their scales
    in the quest   coerced
       by the inevitability
    a red mating   fruitful as trees
    a red death on the river bank
      like apples dropping

iii Schools of fish in pools of fast water
           like seaweed   like ribbons

                painted shawls rippling in water

     dippers   gulls   crows   feeding
                    pomegranate eggs   like eyes

        the salmon sulphur and ruby
           bright-eyed
                      along the river paths

        always the water pulling

                    their couch of gravel
                    the smell of water

                         tingling

In those days music was alive
and danced, schottishe,
polka, minuet,
waltzes to spin the hearts
of giddy girls.

Mary down the street
played piano. Fat fingers
dipped and rolled, blond curls
from setting the night before
softened and grew limp,
perspiration worked crescents
on her wide pink taffeta back
but she couldn't stop.

Arnie played fiddle
out of some Gaelic, Metis,
Irish mist. He stepped
like a heron, all legs and lunch,
but when he struck up
light bounced off the walls,
all the sleeping children
raised their heads.

At those dances
my father played the banjo,
plucked music from a hundred places
to skip around the hall.

When he strummed at home
the evenings sparkled
like the wood fire,
mother busy with the darning,
or the summer twilight listening
at the window.
His songs were there
before we knew of poetry
or love.

And one long summer
my grandmother came to stay.
Quiet evenings, the rowboat,
green reflecting lake.
From the shore we listened.
Grandmother's clear soprano voice,
more perfect than loons.
Father's banjo, settlers moving west
over a continent.

Three people in a boat going downriver,
Lac St. Louis opening before them.
They are low in the water, propelled
more by current than their small engine.
Dark against the hollow sun
the figures could be men or women,
huddled against the river wind.
Someone's washing on the far bank flaps,
only sheets instead of sails.
Yellow leaves hang on branches
taut as clothesline.

Coureurs de bois cherished days like these,
late October, open water, last chance
to run the river into winter haven.
The river is mottled, chop
from the wind, smooth water
polished by the current.
Their journey is measured in bridges,
steeples, three people, men or women,
in the channel moving downstream
intent on some landing further on.
Some memory from the past,
some future hope out of the east,
clouds building over the river.

On Spanish Banks at low tide
green seaweed lies flat against the sand.
It flares out from nodules
like the buried heads of maidens
who stand, patient and enduring,
on the bottom of the sea.

Maidens with green hair,
are you waiting for lovers
in long canoes whose chanting
carried over the water
after the tide had taken them?
Are you here to welcome the Spanish *galetas*
with their silver spoons and silver tongues
who will not return?

Or are you here for some
antique purpose of your own,
perhaps as markers for other women, who
entering strange harbours
look around for signs.
We see you patient,
subdued and beautiful
under the waves.

We are waiting also
but your words are obscure
and difficult. Long ago sand
stopped your tongues.

Under Granville Bridge black ink
pools around heavy pylons; netted
above, roosting starlings, pigeons
are safe in cat-free haven.
Beyond the shadow, bridge lights
splash across the tranquil mesh
of little waves.

Slowly, the ruffle in the water
is stippled with silver flashes,
a school of herring drawn
to long-eroded spawning banks.
Here is the city, the muffled
beat of autos on the bridge
above, the frieze of highrise homes
where forests grew.
A man I knew once fished salmon
from his porch, held up by posts
planted in the inlet sludge.
That was eighty years ago.

It is late, the boaters and the ferries
ceased hours ago. The thick
thrum of motor from the west
looms into a tugboat, its tow a barge
big as a wharf, speeding down the empty
channel as if a ghost were conjured
by the silver herring.
No one lingers on the island.
The bars and restaurants
are closed, the pigeons
tucked down on their red feet
under the bridge. Still water somehow
dreams the herring into a circle of shine,
reflects the memory of salmon, forest
and the long canoes when they paddled
under the waning moon, the channel
split into shakes of radiance.

This afternoon sun lights the bay
with a glare so bright
each opulent cedar branch,
heat-withered alder, red arbutus
crackle with fire.
Stricken, trees fall into water,
a flat sheen of forest
floating the way gasoline
makes rainbows, but this one
all green, a skin of crinkled green
and green beneath, the sun-bent sea
rippling over starfish caverns,
rock pliant as grass.

Salt blood swells and falls,
the sound of shells in the forest.

In the sea, wave-shafts
snap the tinder branches,
flakes of sun and sand
scatter my glass-green fins.
I swim into this forest
under the forest, blossoms
of kelp and fucus in liquid
motion among the quivering shadows.
My own shadow swims under me
as limpid, as cool as a shoal
of fish under ships.

CHANGELING

A vanished summer when
with string and pin he fished
for carp beneath a dock
in shadow-rippled sand
not for food, but for the silver
presence, gloss and scale
pulled from water into light.

A summer when he oared the
dinghy out from shore,
rowed the setting sun along
and caught sea trout
as if his hands were fishes,
wishes even, to make
the sky his own.

Returning late, the lamp
already lit on shore,
he saw a woman slip
out of the sea, her hair
slicked kelp, her eyes
a lure the pursing light
could not explain, a mystery;
he rested on the oars,
a heron in his quiet

and then went in, his fish
forgot, to tell a lie,
that he had seen a seal.

The stars were wrong, a mistake
was made at my birth.
Sleek and fat, only at ease
in salt water, I know
I was meant to be a seal.

There is another seal in our bay
who is not a counterfeit.
He gazes at Julie all day long
while she reads on the rocks,
her long blond hair
languid as sea grass.
The seal watches, rolls and slaps
the blue slick to gain her attention but
Julie merely looks up from her medical text,
returns to her study of human anatomy.

Will Julie one day invent an X-ray
and reveal the thin bones
of my shadow flippers? The lungs
which let me pursue my fish
to the dark sea nests, the
polyp in my brain
balancing, turning my body
in sea arabesques

and the seal's dilemma,
the aborted fingers, toes,
the song which sings like sea water
in rock crevices, but unimaginably
bright and beautiful.
He swirls, thwacks
the water with his flipper,
gains an abstract look from Julie
on the rock. His unmaterialized
human heart thumps
and thumps

At ten o'clock at night this man
is driving across town to bring
to his daughter an old electric fan
and a bag of earth dug
from his compost pile an hour ago
in a circle of flashlight.
The fan is to blow epoxy fumes
from her studio, where
she has been painting props
for a Grade B movie.
The earth is for a clay pot where
in spring she planted a sunflower
in three tea cups of soil.
The flower bloomed once and died,
but now new buds spring up
around the stalk, promise
Indian Summer in the clay pot.

This man is tired, he wants to go
to bed, but he is driving across town
on this September night to bring
to his daughter the autumn air
freshened with scent of mountains.
To bring to her the sun we cause to rise
each morning, in any way we can.

That Clapton clappin' blues beat stringing out the rainy
afternoon, Susan swinging easy and slow, the guitar sweet
enough to turn the sea to treacle, two friends on the slidey
summer air, their feet as gentle as butterfly wings, Dora is
chiffon, Dora is cotton candy, Dora is a mist in the breeze
of a Clapton guitar, Susan is the wind carrying a melody
through green gardens, sinuous and easy as honeysuckle on a
trellis, Dora the perfume of roses in the space between the
notes, the HUMM, HUMM, HUMM, HUMMM, HUMM of honey
bees in the roses, Susan as supple as cedar trees, swaying, swaying,
bare feet plucking the floor, Dora floating on the music like
sunlight on water, the piano notes a staircase to the stars,
Susan and Dora dipping like swallows in the evening sky,
soaring against the new moon, higher and higher, the dusk a
carpet, the dancers as far and bright as the evening star,
see them there beyond the sunset waving a blues goodbye.

I didn't have an easy time of it.
Look, nobody did, so I can't complain.
At least I spoke English,
not like the eyetalians and the frenchies.
Just the same, sometimes I used to wish
I could sit out in the backyard
under a grapevine, the sun shining,
with a glass of wine.
They made it themselves, see
except when the police came,
spilled out all the crocks.
It wasn't legal, then.

The eyetalians were good gardeners,
you could say that for them.
Beautiful dahlias, and vegetables
you wouldn't believe.

Over on our street it was the washing that counted.
All those white sheets on a Monday
and the copper boiler on the wood stove,
hot water, the scrubbing board,
the hard soap and the bluing in the rinse.
Hanging them all out and taking them all in again.
Then, with the wood stove going,
you might as well make pies.

Tuesday was the ironing
and the wood stove hot again
and maybe the windows all steamed up
because it was raining
and the clothes still drying in the kitchen.
Anyway, you needed the stove
for the irons, two of them,
one to heat up and one you slammed
on all those white sheets,
those pillow cases and tea cloths,
underwear and pyjamas
and the shirts for Saturday night.

Jack cut all the firewood in his spare time
and looked after the front lawn,
which was for us the way the dahlias
were for the eyetalians.

Sometimes, when I get to thinking,
I wonder if there is anyone, anywhere
who remembers my white sheets on the clothesline
the way I remember, red and white,
yellow, orange and speckled, like big pom-poms
in the sunshine, those dahlias?

I overhear someone at a party say J- - -
was married three times, but he only ever
mentions two of his wives, and I wonder
about the third wife, did he love her
too much and did she walk out
one day, a grey mist of rain and
the mail lying on the mat under the door,
leaving her umbrella and the children.
He is a man who dresses carefully,
an ascot knotted in his shirt
and soft Italian shoes. Did she
dash away to another woman, something
that corrugates his well-groomed heart,
or is she in the suburbs somewhere,
living with a chartered accountant.
I want to think of her striding
through Peru or Java in boots
and a long silk scarf, the wind blowing
her hair as another sunrise rushes over
the summit of Gunung Slamet. I want to imagine
him in a house kept carefully by a German
cleaning woman. The bathroom exhales
his cologne and his shoes are in a
straight line on his closet floor.
From time to time he picks up a book
with her name on the flyleaf,
that capital S like a swan, or her cool
kiss as she walked out of the sea.

He rings a friend, they drink wine
in a bar where they are admired,
so distingué. He is older, there is
another woman, discreet and handsome.
Her glove size is the same as the shadow
wife, he finds this useful at birthdays,
and tries not to notice that
her hands are dry as bread crumbs.
He believes that they are content together,
they go to lectures and holiday
in France, but when he is convinced
that he is happy, a postcard drops
onto the mat. The terra cotta mermaid,
the sea-green glaze, the long S under
her scrawl "Wonderful country. Hope
you are well" lifts away his house,
his lover, his academic reputation
and he wishes, wishes, wishes
her back onto the doorstep, her hands
outstretched and cool.

I arrive at the house of a woman I know where I
find her watering her plants. She walks slowly
around the room carrying a heavy blue jug with
a chipped rim. She looks at the walls and
chairs as if they were exhibits in a gallery
and does not acknowledge me. "How are you?" I
ask. She stops in the middle of the room, her
weight caught on one foot, her left arm raised
to support the burden of the blue jug. "I have
so many days," she says. The room is dim and
closed, faintly green from the trees outside.
She balances in the middle of the room, the
blue jug and the half-watered plants hold
her there as the light fades to pallid shadow.

Along the horse path, a mother and small boy on bicycles,
their heads buckled into helmets like boxers
(but ears free, to hear the horses).
The tide is running high in the river, the path thick
with sawdust and rotted manure, the lagoon
opaque and green.

Fishes are lying in the deep mud bottoms, earless,
listening with their fins to the rising tide,
to the sun setting in a noiseless crescendo.

The small boy listens for horses with his eyes.
Shadows are moving on the river,
on the surface of trees. He listens with his eyes
while the shadows shy and toss.

They become strange, forget
the ties that bound them to
a familiar world, forget their
underwear, their brassieres, their
                    bodies
demanding comfort now, after the
fierce holding of appearances, family,
all the animate world, on course:
pilots who must navigate over
mountain ridges, vast oceans.

At last they furl their sails,
undo the lines. Their bodies
lose shape, their skin shrivels,
they moor themselves to the walls
of small rooms, appear to sleep.
Sometimes in the dark, their
bodies shiver, the slight motion
of a chrysalis in winter.

My festival clothes: rose-spangled blouse,
sea-green skirt, are folded
smooth on the bedroom chair.
Out in the dark strait a boat

speeds the night. Too early yet
another summer dawn. Alone,
the boat and rider are bound
to me by the thin sound of engine.

A few drops spatter
on the roof. You are among the trees,
rain ice-cold on the mountain.
Is it man or woman in the boat,
how far to go, how many fathoms of sea

beneath? My small light webs
the mountain with the water,
the boat with my folded dress,
red roses, on the chair.

*   *   *

The bay is quiet, the tide pulls
gently at the rocky land. A hand
persuasive at first, and then denied
lets go crab nests of seaweed,
starfish clusters of operatic colour.

When the sun rises, confident
as eagles, the barnacles
and anemones shutter among the rocks,
become another kingdom, another rule.

*   *   *

In this country, Kingfisher is grey,
the colour of clouds and uncertain water,
how the squalls darken, their shadows
threaten the fisherfolk, and the quick
speedboat heading for a further cove.

Who is Wizard of this shifting zone,
the water never still: even when its cast
is smooth opal, underneath it moves
and clutches, a shadow of that shift
within the boiling earth.

Azure is another philosophy
less stern, the rule of sparkling light.
Kingfisher here knows survival
like his carnivorous prey, how fast
to grasp; the grey rain casts spells,
circles under the Wizard's perch.

*   *   *

In this place, a woman can become
crystal and know that it is good.
The song of the winter wren
and the spring aria of eagles
are changed to rose quartz.

Lichens crust in sunlight,
melt in rain as if stone wore
its heart on the outside, its
crumbling long and slow and calm
beside wild summer roses.

Waiting and meditation
are the work of stones,
the future grows upon us
like moss. Only listen,
love is the raven's shadow.

GARMENTS OF LIGHT

Let us go into the desert
there to live, a tent
of parachute silk, our spare
bodies in that narrow space.
Through gleaming heat
the white shape hovers, sails
on furrows of sand.
Each night the frozen stars
beckon, not touching
under the knife of God.

Once you left me in the desert
alone, a few sticks for my fire,
bleak waste for cheer.
Only the steppe falcon, a shriek
in the sky, and a shadow
out of the west, blown sand
under the hooves of two horses.

I stood as the men rode in,
their saddle cloths kilim
bright as mosque tiles.
Behind, the dead hares
hung down, and their rifles
on saddle and thigh.
What was my need? one asked
as he held his horse to my camp.
None, I replied,
face to face with sky.
God keep you, he said.
They swung and were gone.
Smoke from my fire, scuffed sand
and the gift of the horsemen
unasked for, open and sudden
as light.

I FOLLOW MY BODY LIKE A PATH

(it is mapped in nerves, in small
bones, webbed veins
difficult to read)

persuasive the path, voices
calling, exploits tender
and daring

the rhythm of blood
of open roads, the sun a gong.
Each minute a swallow, each day
as permanent as Roman milestones

the path, at last, relentless
adventures unanticipated, hard places
cracked bones, bruises blooming at dusk

footsteps on the trail ahead.
A stranger walking in the forest.
I place my feet in unfamiliar spaces

follow

This is the chir pine
and this is the song of the whistling-thrush
at first light. A black pye-dog
rummages across the lawn.

The winter dust line smudges out
the plains, a mile below.
It is the beginning of March. Green
creeps over the arid soil.

Last night we watched two golden-
backed woodpeckers and a pair of owls.
The owls called out from a deodar tree
who, whoooooooo, whowhoooooooooo.

Soon it will be spring, bird song
and flowers scattered as if for a god.
Tubs on the lawn filled with geraniums,
scarlet minivets flitting in the pines.

When the whistling-thrush sings
at dusk from the chir I will be
a clear space without sound or shadow,
no winged bird to return me here.

After, I followed you along
the old path. It had rained all night,
it was like walking in the shallows

of a clear lake.
Salal leaves became silver,
mosses surged with rain water.

On the side of the path,
away from the footprints and the mud,
earthworms stretched themselves out,

strands of old lavender-coloured ribbon
as long as my hand, travelling
on the left as if admonished

by a cautious parent. I stepped
carefully over the water-driven
migrants. Once, the worms moved

dumbly through fallen salmonberry
petals, exotic pink. All the distance
of the path I considered this exile

brought on by rain, how we travel
unknowingly to something
farther down the road.

When I emerged from the forest,
I was soaked by water dropping
from the trees, oozing from the dark

mud under my feet. The air glistened.
In the clearing, your shadow
was already evaporating,

sunlight caught in the treetops.

A FEW WORDS TO OMAR KHAYYAM

*

Is it real, this wilderness
you speak of, clothed
with singing larks and vines?
You do not say what metaphor
describes this place, identifies
the map where a clear hand
has written out the path.
We have searched for centuries,
search each morning by a final star
but cannot find it. Guided
by your music we move on
perplexed and hopeful, although
the desert hawk curls overhead
and water is an empty word.

**

A clay cup brimming with red wine
is all we are, you say: earth
and blood embarked upon a sleep
as old as yours.

An easy thought, that scattered
petals fall from roses
and we the passive watch.
The catch is this. Each time
the rivers lose their way,
each time the sleeping forest
finds that age is not enough,
each time the birds return
to barren ridges, empty skies
our names are written down.
The pen moves on, and in the ledger
of iniquity we cannot cancel
half a line.

Legend says this city
rose like a woman from the water,
wheat fields tugging at her skirts.
On the street today Turkish women
walk in folded shalvar which
flow about them like sea waves.

Men who talked to God
built great mosques with jewelled minarets.
They lie now in tiled tombs among
fields of painted flowers.
Even their brothers in nearby
graveyards wear turbaned headstones
as mark of rank and station.
Each twist and fold of cloth
is cut in hard white marble.

Among the tombstones
a woman and her children gather
twigs to start the evening fire.
Their worn garments move around them
murmuring to God.

CARAVAN

Under poplars at the edge
of an Anatolian field
three shepherds sit,
their cloaks thrown back
on the unplanted stubble

a simple meal, olives
goat's cheese, hearth-baked bread
wrapped in homespun cloth

each day they do this,
two old men and a boy,
each day have done so
as their fathers
and grandfathers before
broke bread together

as, long ago, Paul
journeying from Tarsus
with the slow camel train,
sleeping in caravanserai
against the wolves and wind,
saw them here

sat down among them under
poplar shelter, the sun
burning the zenith overhead

and the shepherds asked,
"Teacher, where is God?"

Paul, remembering what he
had himself learned, replied
"Each time we take food
together, remember that God
is here among us,
remember that God also is in
the rough taste of shared bread."

Outside the door of the Benedictine chapel
wheat scattered on the floor.
Squash, pumpkins, carrots, jars of preserves

wild flowers, blue, on a bundle of hay.

The north wind blows,
throws snow at the sky.
Howls through the dark spruce windbreak
the window chinks.

Snow in the furrows of plowed fields.
The last tomatoes, cucumbers, ungleaned
yield to gods of decay.

The horizon is not a place
you want to go to.

If your heart is somewhere else,
how do you keep warm?

Sun lies sickly in a bed of cloud
without bird song or dancing,
darkness is in the ascendant:

> the wheel is turning, turning.
> You know the story, the light
> at the end of the tunnel, Persephone
> at the end of her dream. But these are old
> myths, can you trust them one more time?

What can you trust?

This, perhaps. Blue flowers
on a bundle of hay.

The spurt of your candle sent
yellow light glinting slant-eyed,
the grin of one last tooth,
you old Lucifer, beckoning
to the child on the front stairs.

You are not immortal, devil,
here on the back porch you sink
into rot, an old man's face,
lips loose and puffed, eyes
folding over the bridge of your nose.
Your dry stem curls into one last
noose of hair.

See, a squirrel has been eating
your skull cap, a serrated edge
of tooth marks, scattered
bits of flesh. All Saints Day
is gone, devil, your resurrection
lies in the compost heap,
a few seeds, rotting squash.

Old devil, what can you offer
now to the child's expectation
as winter comes on,
another light in the dark?

After dinner we left the bread, the wine glasses,
the red and purple mats, the napkins
crumpled on the table. She led us through
a sodden field. Under our feet grass seeped
cold as the out-going winter tides.

The night was a low black cloud, one
dark gloom of pool, and once the flash
of neighbouring Christmas lights,
too far to break the alder palisade.

The sheep pens were lit penuriously,
shadows and empty bins encompassed
in a dreary hollow. And then she asked
why owls did not come here.

You told her coons and coyotes hazard
such a place, even this wide shelter
under the shingled eave. It was a dream,
sheep fat with wool on summer
grass, muscovy ducks, the cats
stalking mice in sweet hay nests.

That farm is as distant as the far-off
Christmas lights. We start back,
a stable empty of animals or any living thing
while rain begins, on Christmas night.

"Neither were there no pets for God, No dogs either."

(Alex, three years old, telling a story)

But in a heaven without animals, what is there for God,
what relaxation, what enjoyment, what tenderness?
No sticky dog salival slatherings, no cockatoo resting its
waxy head in the palm of his hand. Cats with gifts of
mice, crickets hiding in the folds of his robe, bantam
roosters, earthworms, striped snakes, salamanders, crabs
and tadpoles in jam jars, rabbits, goldfish, a choir of
canaries, a banality of budgerigars, God peacefully raking
the leaves in the garden, at twilight closing the hen house,
singing to the elephant's baby. The orangutan nestles in
the tree tops, a few leaves falling. Tired and content, God
settles into his armchair, gathers up a small child, reads
"Old MacDonald Had a Farm" one more time. Listen,
he says, to the vespers of the hermit thrush. Bats and
nighthawks fly out of his hair.

Sometimes you can go
too far, travelling out
from the centre to the sharp
confines of nothing. Air and sky
tear the body's balance,
pluck out the crosshairs
of certainty.

Beyond Simla, beyond
Narkanda, into the edge
of the High Himalayas,
the army road to Tibet
cuts, a knife blade of highway
tracking the Sutlej River.

Three fierce days on the road,
now you sleep in a hut
under piled blankets,
under slate roof tiles
heavy as thunder.

On a morning without
sunrise, you climb
slowly to a rock ledge:
five thousand feet below
a wooden bridge crosses
to Tibet. You cannot
look   down
there is nothing to hold
onto as you turn away.
Your legs are snow.

A Pahari woman from
lowland meadows, bent
with her bundle of grasses,
comes along the path
too narrow to pass.
The woman steps out beyond
the precipice, turns
like a falcon in air.

Now the silence is an open
knife, you are suspended
on the tip of the blade
while the Sutlej River
flows through the gorge.
The woman has vanished
on the trail ahead.

Everywhere they are listening.
Among the lilacs at the gate their ears
wait tenderly for your voice.
Their fingers are in the water
as you reach down from the rowboat
to the cool green sea.

On the cliffs of summer
where sea wind dances with yellow daisies
they whisper, whisper in the dry moss.

From the long ridge of Sanjauli
where in the Anglican cemetery white stones
are toppled by hands or time and the great birds
circle glades of ancient pleasures,
they remember their garments of light.

In the small graveyards of the new world
where they brought their hopes
and their cradle songs, you know
they are in the silence of the moon
and in the newly mowed grass.

The stories we are telling now
are the stories they are waiting for
eagerly, without bone or breath.
Molecules of air which once were theirs
and now, like heirloom pearls, are ours
resound with the new long ago,
freshly-fashioned words of our mouth.
Words, kisses, bones.
We each sing this song once
here, among the living. We each listen
to the other voices, the other chorus
in our dreams and in the early morning.

MADONNA OF THE STAIRS

Muenster, Saskatchewan

The students jostle in the corridor
books under their arms,
the winter light from the windows
hard, like bottle glass.
At the end of the corridor
an unlit corner
unnoticed by the kids:
Michaelangelo's
Madonna of the Stairs.

> *all air here   shadowed*
> *hollowed out   a halo*
> *of silence reverberating*
> *intrinsic*

Born at Caprese in Tuscany
he was the age of these kids,
trembled with the same vigour.
At sixteen, adopted by Lorenzo
the Magnificent. Lodged
in the Palazzo de Medici,
Via Largo.

not palazzo stairs   only
a common passageway
any mother sitting with her child
held in her lap
still half part of the same flesh
wrapped in the same embracing
garment

but a particularity
the child leaning in
away from the rumble of history
while the thick Tuscan boy
reaches over the wall
winds a width of cloth

the other children play
unwatched by mother and child
her static reverie
his turned away face

At sixteen, Mary answered
when the Angel of the Annunciation
summoned her.

her face looks inward
back to the angel in the garden
incandescent   omnipotent

forward to the burden
God has imposed on her
humble knowledge of death

her shoulders are like oxen
her hands are strong as spades
one foot turned over   the arch
a house for sorrow

He sucked the passion for sculpture,
the blooming stone, he said,
with his mother's milk.
Dignity and pain in heavy stone.

the child leans against
his mother's silence
one hand turned back
a fingered shell
a new vessel for water

Michaelangelo the Great.
Mary of the Sorrows.
These young kids jostle
their way to a hockey game.

At the end of the corridor
the wall   waits.

the Tuscan boy
folds a winding sheet

the mother is wrapped
in desire and foreboding

stone within the rippling
garment like the sea

P. 12. Turkish. The child calls "Anne": mother. The woman sings "Canım": my heart, or sweetheart. The "c" in "Canım" is pronounced as a "j" in English.

P. 34. Shallal. The name of this common west coast shrub is generally written and pronounced "salal." However the Gage Canadian Dictionary says of it, "a small evergreen shrub (*Gaultheria shallon*) native to the Pacific coast, having glossy leaves, showy white flowers and edible purplish berries [Chinook Jargon (klkwu)-shala]." At one time on parts of the B.C. coast, the name of the shrub was pronounced "shallal," which was probably closer to the Chinook.

P. 49. Tree rings. For Marion Parker, dendrochronologist and forest preservationist. Marion argued early that the remaining ancient forests of the West Coast are irreplaceable and should no longer be cut down. From tree stumps on the summit of the Sechelt Peninsula north of Vancouver, he documented tree ring sequences exceeding 1,840 years. Residual stands nearby contain the world's oldest living trees in closed canopy forests. Marion Parker died in June 1999.

ACKNOWLEDGMENTS

Some of these poems have appeared in the following journals and anthologies: *Amythyst Review, CV2, Event, Grain, Green Fuse, New Orphic Review, Room of One's Own, TickleAce, Witness to Wilderness: the Clayoquot Sound Anthology*; and in *Flames and Courtesy* (Hawthorne Society Chapbook series). "Listening" was published as a broadside by High Ground Press, Madeira Park, B.C.

I am grateful to the writers who have read some of these poems, and to George McWhirter and members of the poetry seminar in the Creative Writing Department at UBC. Many thanks also to my editor, Nathalie Cooke.

And always, Paul.